Explaining Catholic Teaching on Marriage, Separation & Divorce

by
Jane Deegan

All booklets are published thanks to the generous support of the members of the Catholic Truth Society

CATHOLIC TRUTH SOCIETY
PUBLISHERS TO THE HOLY SEE

2

Contents

All rights reserved. First published 2012 by The Incorporated Catholic Truth Society, 40-46 Harleyford Road London SE11 5AY Tel: 020 7640 0042 Fax: 020 7640 0046. Copyright © 2012 The Incorporated Catholic Truth Society.

ISBN 978 1 86082 806 5

Front cover image: *Holding hands with a ring* © Stefan Kunz/ imagebroker/Corbis. *Inside pictures: The Holy Trinity* by Andrei Rublev © The Gallery Collection/Corbis; *Detail of Christ and Apostle in The Last Supper from the Refectory of the Abbey of Pomposa* © Araldo de Luca/CORBIS.

Introduction

The Catholic Church teaches that a valid sacramental marriage, once consummated, can never be dissolved. To understand why the Church teaches that divorce is not permissible is to understand in the first instance that she cannot teach anything else, for this teaching does not come from her but from the most Blessed Holy Trinity, from God himself revealed to us in Jesus Christ.[1]

This booklet will seek to explain the words of Christ about divorce. It will describe the fallen human condition and sin, which underlies divorce, but equally it will proclaim and explain the good news of redemption in Jesus Christ and what that means for love and marriage. It will explain why a relationship with Jesus Christ enables us to draw on the grace we need in order to remain faithful to wedding vows, and it will discuss some of the obstacles that couples can put in the way of grace. It will examine the importance of understanding the spiritual battle in which Christians are engaged and ways in which we can easily be deceived into taking a different path to that of the Gospel. It will look at the influence and effect of alternative world views which have taken their toll on the hearts and minds of many of the faithful, weakening faith or arresting its growth. It will also look at the tragic and devastating impact of divorce on the children of the family. Finally it will look at the teaching of the Church with regard to separation, divorce and remarriage outside the Church; the difference between valid and invalid marriages, the meaning of the Pauline and Petrine privileges and the meaning of the "internal forum" solution.

The Word of the Lord

God is the creator of man and woman and of marriage.
God himself instituted marriage in the beginning, and from
the beginning he had a plan and a purpose for doing so that
was ordered to the happiness and fulfilment of man and
woman. All of us, deep down, have a need to know the
truth,[2] because happiness can only be found in the truth.
The truth is powerful even if it is sometimes painful and
not what we want to hear. Truth is something objective,
not subjective as many would like us to believe. It is not
the same as opinion - 'my truth' as opposed to 'your
truth'.[3] Subjective truth is only *the truth* when it adheres
to objective truth, to the way in which God has ordained
things. Objective truth is discoverable by us by virtue of
reason and revelation.[4] Christ told us that he came into
the world to bear witness to the truth and that the truth
will set us free.[5] Further, he said that all who are on the
side of truth listen to his voice.[6] What, then, is the truth
concerning divorce, and why do many couples decide that
it is the only way forward?

> "Some Pharisees approached him, and to test him they
> said, 'Is it against the Law for a man to divorce his
> wife on any pretext whatever?' He answered, 'Have

you not read that the creator from the beginning made them male and female and that he said: This is why a man must leave his father and mother, and cling to his wife, and the two become one body? They are no longer two, therefore, but one body. So then, what God has united, man must not divide.' They said to him, 'Then why did Moses command that a writ of dismissal should be given in cases of divorce?' 'It was because you were so unteachable,' he said 'that Moses allowed you to divorce your wives, but it was not like this from the beginning.'[7]

Back at the Beginning

To begin to unravel what Christ is really saying here and what he means, we must in the first instance go back with him to the beginning. This will help us to understand what marriage was like when God first created man and woman and gave them to each other. The truth about who we are as human beings exists in a state of tension, between how we were originally created to be, how we discover ourselves with our fallen human nature or sinfulness (wounded, but not totally corrupted, by original sin) and what it means to be redeemed in Christ.

Many people find Genesis difficult and are tempted perhaps to consider that they have "come of age", so to speak, and that because the cause and reason for our existence

The Holy Trinity by Andrei Rublev

can now be interpreted in other ways, perhaps by the theory of evolution or some other scientific explanation, Genesis must now be redundant because these other reasonings appear to contradict it.

Genesis was never intended to be a scientific account; it provides a completely different kind of explanation and it contains ancient truth[8] which is as relevant today as when it was first written. We can only know God through what he chooses to reveal to us,[9] and since we are made in his image and likeness, unless we come to know God we cannot truly and fully know or understand ourselves.[10] The Scriptures are part of God's revelation to us about who he is and who we really are, where we have come from and where we are going. We cannot therefore disregard them if we are in search of the true meaning of our lives, or the true meaning of love and marriage, or if we are to understand why divorce is gravely wrong. Furthermore, the Word of God is alive and active; it has the power to bring about what it proclaims to those who are open and willing to receive it.[11]

Let us take a look, then, at what God intended by instituting marriage in the beginning, by taking a closer look at the account in Genesis; this will help us to understand why Christ says what he does about divorce. There are two accounts, one in which God creates man and woman simultaneously and the other where he creates the man first. We will be looking primarily at the latter. In both accounts God created everything that exists through love. Everything he created bore his mark, so to speak, and was a gift; but only man and woman were created in his image and likeness: "Let us make man in our own image". In the account in which God creates the man (male) first, only man (as the first human being) could understand that everything created was by way of a gift, including his own being, and only he could respond to God with gratitude and love, which indeed he did. God was for him a loving father with whom he experienced a loving relationship.[12]

God tells him to name the animals and in doing so he discovers that he is different from them. He has self-consciousness and a freedom that they do not share. He can choose freely what to do and what not to do, whereas their freedom is limited and they are governed primarily by instinct. It was in fact his body that in part revealed this to him, since he discovered that he could use his body in a unique way in comparison to them, for example he could "cultivate [the earth] and take care of it" whereas they could not. He discovers that he has spiritual gifts of intellect and freedom that they do not have.

Although made in the image and likeness of God, man is not equal to God; God is creator and man is a creature. In dialogue with God he discovers therefore that his freedom is not unlimited; God tells him of the tree of the knowledge of good and evil and that he can eat of all the trees in the garden, but of the fruit of that tree he may not eat; if he does he will die. Before this tree he is called to halt, for "God who alone is good, knows perfectly what is good for man, and by virtue of his love proposes this good to man in the commandments".[13]

The Original Meaning of Love and Marriage

Man discovers that what determines who he is, is to a greater extent something invisible, that is, his spiritual gifts, his soul. Outwardly, he may be similar to the animals, but he is not like them; among them, consequently, he could not find his equal: he could not find a true companion. As man comes to realise this, God as his loving Father articulates it for him: "It is not good that the man should be alone".[14] If man is made in God's image then he must be made with a capacity for love and communion. God does not exist alone; he exists as a Trinity of three Divine Persons in a communion of love.

God therefore puts the man into a deep sleep and takes a rib from his side from which he fashions woman. He gives the woman and the man to each other. The man for the first time experiences being able to transcend himself; he experiences being able to go out from himself towards another. He experiences what it means to love, to relate to and to be in relationship with another. This is a fundamental aspect of the mystery of the Holy Trinity. God is the mystery of three Divine Persons in relationship: a relationship of love. God is *being in relation*. We too, then, are only persons by virtue of our ability to be in relationship with each other and to love each other. We image God when we live in true and loving relation and communion[15].

> "God is love and in himself he lives a mystery of personal loving communion. Creating the human race in his own image and continually keeping it in being, God inscribed in the humanity of man and woman the vocation, and thus the capacity and responsibility, of love and communion. Love is therefore the fundamental and innate vocation of every human being."[16]

At a foundational level, man and woman exist in a union and communion in their common humanity, since no man or woman alone can represent the human race, only man and woman together - the unity of the two, equal but different. This first level of union and communion between them therefore is as brother and sister, a virginal communion in their common humanity. From this level of union God calls them to a more specific form of communion, that of marriage. The marital relationship is a unique form of such communion which includes their entire being; body and soul, "they become one body"[17] in their complimentary differentiation.

On seeing the woman and loving her, the man understands himself more deeply. Until that moment his sexuality had been asleep, so to speak, but now in front

of her an awakening begins. Her femininity helps him
understand his masculinity, he understands himself to be a
man and her a woman. She is like him in that she is a person
with spiritual gifts, but she is different; for example she is
built differently and he sees that their bodies are designed
to fit together, that they can become one flesh. Their bodies
have not been randomly designed but are sacramental. As
man and woman, their bodies have a spousal or nuptial
meaning or significance. Their bodies make visible an
invisible truth: that man and woman are created through
love, for love. Genesis then says: "This is why a man
leaves his father and mother and joins himself to his wife,
and they become one body."[18] Marriage thereby comes
into being. Love is the primary vocation of every human
person; it is written, one might say, into our very DNA.

> "Man cannot live without love. He remains a being that
> is incomprehensible for himself, his life is senseless, if
> love is not revealed to him, if he does not encounter
> love, if he does not experience it and make it his own, if
> he does not participate intimately in it."[19]

The love they experience for each other emotionally
and spiritually through the conjoining of their souls can
expressed physically as man and wife through their bodies.
"God blessed them, saying to them, 'Be fruitful, multiply".[20]
Into the gift of marital sexual love and communion God has
placed the gift of fertility and procreation. The communion

of husband and wife in the sexual embrace, through which the two become one flesh, open to new life in their child, is the human communion of three persons in a communion of love. Man and woman are embodied spirits, whereas God is pure spirit, which means that the human communion of love in marriage, which includes their bodies, is something new in his creation, peculiar to man, created male and female:

> "As an incarnate spirit, that is a soul which expresses itself in a body and a body informed by an immortal spirit, man is called to love in his unified totality. Love includes the human body, and the body is made a sharer in spiritual love."[21]

Simultaneously it makes present something of the mystery of true love that is in God. "Married love particularly reveals its true nature and nobility when we realize that it takes its origin from God, who 'is love', the Father 'from whom every family in heaven and on earth is named'."[22]

So, because human marital and familial love and communion come from God, reflect God's love and involve God's action in procreation, marriage and the marital sexual act are holy. The love, truth and beauty of marriage and family were originally intended to point us to the love and communion that God invites us to shaer with him for all eternity. Throughout the Scriptures, both Old and New Testaments, the image of marital love and relationship is an image often used by God to reveal his intimate love for his people and the love between Christ and his bride the Church.

Let us look a little closer, then, at the love experienced between the first couple. Adam loves and receives the woman as a gift, as a person, for her own sake. This is his response to her making a gift of herself to him. He sees her whole person, body and soul. In being received and loved for herself for her own sake in this way, Eve truly finds herself. She experiences who she truly is and in that experience finds happiness and joy. Adam makes a gift of himself to her in return and she receives him in the same way in all purity, simplicity and innocence. In so doing he too truly finds himself, he is enriched by the experience and he too discovers the depth of his person, and of his masculinity; through which experience he too finds true happiness and joy. "Man…cannot truly find himself except through a sincere gift of himself".[23]

This is how love and marriage were in the beginning. The love of the first couple, their giving and receiving of each other so perfectly, was only possible because it was born out of their relationship with God who they knew and loved as Father, upon whom they depended for everything, in whom they trusted and whom they obeyed. They had given their *fiat* to God - let all that you have ordained be so; they had accepted everything he had given in love as gift, everything as he had ordained it to be and they had responded with gratitude and love. This remains a prerequisite; it is the foundation of all human love. Without this right relationship with God as Father, it is not possible for us truly to experience human love as it was designed to be. The two most important commandments therefore are no longer perceived as arbitrary rules but more as the blueprint of who we really are: persons created in the beginning in the image and likeness of God. Their love was holy, pure and innocent and thus they were naked without shame.

> "'You must love the Lord your God with all your heart, with all your soul, and with all your mind'…The second resembles it: 'you must love your neighbour as yourself.'"[24]

We yearn to love in this way and be so loved; we yearn for the inner integrity that enables us to love the other for who they are, exactly as they are, and to be loved in the same way, not just to love and be loved when it suits us or when our spouse is useful to us or making us happy according to our own definition or design for happiness. Most couples who get married have touched or experienced something of this, which is why they get married in the first place. How we were originally created to be still subsists within us at a very deep level, because we were wounded but not totally corrupted by sin. Deep down beneath all our personal sins, beneath the wound of original sin, like an echo, like the negative of a photograph, the model of how God originally created us to be still subsists. The experience of true love is one of the ways in which we touch this reality within us. However, true love proves evasive; it seems to slip through our fingers, and we can seem powerless to grasp it and hold onto it or to sustain it out of our own strength.

Original Sin and its Consequences
- the Cause of Divorce

Why is this? What went wrong? What were and are the consequences of sin? The serpent tempted Eve to doubt God's love for her. He tempted her to believe that God was not a loving Father, but rather that he was cheating her and Adam in some way by not allowing them to eat the fruit of the tree of knowledge of good and evil. He tempted her to believe that if they did do so they would not die; rather they would truly be like him, they would "be like gods"[25], able to discern good from evil.

They took and ate.

Immediately their eyes were opened and they realised they were naked. They had been naked without shame, but now they experienced shame. This is because listening to and believing the lie of the serpent meant rejecting the love and communion they had enjoyed with God as Father. As they doubted God and rejected the truth about him, they ceased to be able to experience the power of his Spirit within them. They discovered that they were now afraid of God in the wrong way and were tempted to hide from him.[26]

> "In that sin man preferred himself to God…he chose himself over and against God, against the requirements of creaturely status and therefore against his own good…Seduced by the devil, he wanted to 'be like God', but without God, before God, and not in accordance with God."[27]

Where the love of God and each other had filled their hearts, now *the self* takes centre stage. The emptiness and alienation they experience as a consequence causes them great anguish.

They experience a deep need to escape from it. Threefold lust enters; lust of the eyes, lust of the flesh and pride of life. They experience a fracture of their inner integrity; no longer do their higher spiritual faculties have command over their lower ones:

> "In fact, this seems to be the rule, that every single time I want to do good it is something evil that comes to hand. In my inmost self I dearly love God's Law, but I can see that my body follows a different law that battles against the law which my reason dictates."[28]

Original sin wounded our capacity for self-mastery, and thereby our capacity to love truly, to make a sincere gift of ourselves and to enter into loving communion.

The mastery that God gave to man over creation in the beginning[29] is realised first of all as mastery within his own self.[30] Whereas before when they gazed upon each other they saw the other person in their entirety, body and soul, now it becomes possible for them to see just the body of the other in isolation, and also to view it as an object to be used for the sake of their own personal gratification. Through concupiscence they discover that it is possible for them to experience the body and sex in an impoverished way, disconnected from its true meaning and significance and especially from its spiritual aspect.[31] They are no longer easily able to see the other as a person to be loved. They experience shame because they know deep down they are made for love not use, and they cover their bodies to defend themselves from the inappropriate gaze of the other. They automatically seek to defend the true meaning of their bodies, the spousal nuptial meaning of their physical sexual differentiation. We still respond in this way; if we are surprised by another whilst naked, we automatically cover ourselves, especially if the other person is of the opposite sex.

Their union and communion are now threatened by a different kind of mutual relationship based on lust, domination and mutual recrimination.[32] The possibility of the domination of the woman by the man replaces his reciprocal gift of self and impoverishes them both.[33] In addition, their mutual complementarity, which enriched them in the beginning, now becomes a source of antagonism. The *Catechism* reminds us that this disorder does not stem from the nature of man and woman, or from the nature of their relations, but from sin.[34]

This is the human condition, the condition of fallen human nature. Each one of us will have experienced something of love or its opposite, will have experienced good and evil at the hands of others, and, equally, we will ourselves have been the perpetrators of the same. We restlessly seek happiness but it proves elusive.[35] Our capacity for sinfulness, our limited ability to love and forgive, the effect of the threefold concupiscence that subjugates us to the pleasure of the senses, covetousness for earthly goods, and self-assertion contrary to the dictates of reason,[36] mean that for many of us our relationships can all too easily suffer breakdown. It is sin, therefore, that is the cause of the hardening of hearts that Christ speaks of in his reply to the Pharisees. It is this sin and the consequent hardening of hearts that is the cause of divorce.

"Every man experiences evil around him and within himself. This experience makes itself felt in the relationship between man and woman. Their union has always been threatened by discord, a spirit of domination, infidelity, jealously and conflicts that can escalate into hatred and separation."[37]

The First Promise and the Gift of Hope

God did not abandon the first married couple and neither does he abandon us. He came looking for them in the garden and he comes looking for us. He called them to come out from where they were hiding, and he says the same to us. He wanted to speak with them, and he wants to speak to us. The truth is that the snake was and is *the father of lies,* he who lied to the first couple and has continued to lie ever since. The fact is that God is a loving Father, and his love is essential to our happiness and our ability to love each other. God spoke to Adam and Eve and, after explaining the consequences of their sins, he made them a promise: that he would not leave them in their disordered state but would save them; he would deliver them from sin and death. This, the "Protoevangelium" or "first Gospel", is announced, and from that moment salvation history begins, culminating with the fulfilment of that promise with the annunciation, birth, death and resurrection of Jesus Christ.

Marriage as a Sacrament

Despite the consequences of sin for love and for male-female relations, marriage was still reverenced throughout the Old Testament. True love, although "habitually threatened" by concupiscence, was not completely suffocated;[38] the order of creation subsisted although seriously disturbed.[39] The blessing of God on the original couple passed down from one generation to the next by way of marriage; marriage and family therefore was held in high esteem in the Old Testament. The Church teaches us that marriage in and of itself, after the fall, helps a couple to overcome self-absorption, egoism and the pursuit of selfishness, since it presents the opportunity to open oneself to another, to mutual aid and to self-giving.[40] But because of the reality of sin that lives in us the Church proclaims that marriage is ordained for its fulfilment in Christ and will always stand in need of his healing power:

> "The Church is deeply convinced that only by the acceptance of the Gospel are the hopes that man legitimately places in marriage and in the family capable of being fulfilled. Willed by God in the very act of creation, marriage and the family are interiorly ordained to fulfilment in Christ and have need of his graces in

order to be healed from the wounds of sin and restored to their 'beginning' that is, to full understanding and the full realization of God's plan."[41]

Sin brings separation and isolation, whereas Christ brings unity, wholeness and healing. Divorce belongs to the order of sin, not to the order of creation or of redemption.

Through redemption Christ reversed the effects of original sin. Jesus Christ restores us to his Father,[42] he re-opens heaven for us, he sets us free from our slavery to sin and he restores to us the gift of the Holy Spirit who leads us and guides us to all truth. The Holy Spirit empowers us to live beyond our own strength, to love and to forgive, to be compassionate and long-suffering. We are called to holiness, to discipleship, to enter the household of God. Christ through his death and resurrection restores to us all that was lost through original sin, and gives us even more; he and his Father come to make their home in us. Christian marriage is indissoluble because Christ reversed the effects of sin that leads to divorce and raised marriage to the dignity of a sacrament. As a sacrament, marriage now symbolises and makes present Christ's bond with his bride the Church. When a couple enter into sacramental marriage, Christ takes up their love into his own indissoluble love, and it is this sacramental action that makes the bond between man and wife thus indissoluble. The sacrament opens to the couple channels of grace.

"Marriage, in the new law…by means of Christ confers grace…[Christ merited] the grace that brings natural love to perfection…and sanctifies the spouses."[43]

The sacrament has two levels, one visible and the other invisible, one natural and the other supernatural. The visible is the consent given by both spouses on their wedding day and affirmed in the physical act of self-giving in the consummation of the marriage: this act affirms the vows that have been already verbally expressed. This is to say that the marital sexual act is the total gift of self, a total gift made freely, faithfully, excluding all others and open to life. The invisible level is intertwined with the giving of the verbal consent and the physical consummation of the marriage "and the two shall become one body", since from the moment the latter takes place the marriage is thenceforward indissoluble.[44]

Christ does not leave couples who enter into sacramental marriage to fulfil their vows by their own strength; they are enabled to do so by his power, his strength and his love.[45] Marriage as a sacrament instituted by Christ therefore imparts grace; it is a channel between the souls of the couple and the graces poured forth by our Lord on the cross. It infuses the soul with God's grace. His grace enables us to do or not to do what by our own strength would be impossible. Even if only one of the couple believes, their spouse will be sanctified by the believing husband or wife.[46]

Detail of Christ and Apostle in The Last Supper
from the Refectory of the Abbey of Pomposa

Marriage as a sacrament is efficacious; that is, it brings about what it signifies. It is the way of salvation from that moment on for both husband and wife.[47] The couple can no longer be spiritually separated; they remain married until death parts them. Even if they physically separate and obtain a civil divorce, they remain married in the eyes of God and in the eyes of the Church. If they enter into another relationship whilst their spouse still lives, they become adulterers.

The Good News

Jesus says what he does to the Pharisees because he is the Christ who delivers us from sin; he is the offspring of the woman who crushes the head of the serpent, as promised in the Protoevangelium announced to Adam and Eve; the one who heals us, who takes from our body the heart of stone and replaces it with a heart of flesh. The inevitable consequence of sin that causes the hardening of hearts, that bears fruit in divorce, can therefore end with his coming. This is the good news. To say that divorce should still be permitted is to be incredulous in front of the empty tomb; it is tantamount to saying that Christ has not risen and refusing to believe. Christ is risen, he is risen indeed and he sends to us his Spirit, the Spirit that enables us to cry "Abba, Father", that enables us to forgive and to love and to remain married until death.

"If anyone says that marriage is not truly and properly one of the seven sacraments of the law of the Gospel, and says that it was not instituted by Christ, but introduced into the Church by men, and that it does not confer grace, let him be anathema."[48]

Husband and wife are called to draw strength for their marriage from their individual relationship with Christ, and it is this that will enable them to love and serve each other: "Give way to one another in obedience to Christ".[49] As explained earlier, Adam and Eve were able to love each other so well because of their personal *fiat* to God their Father and their relationship of love with him. We are re-united with the Father through Jesus Christ. It is in and through him, therefore, that we will find the possibility to love and forgive and for our love to be sustained. All marriages will encounter difficulties; Christ does not promise us a trouble free life[50] and in fact the difficulties are part of the journey. Transformation in Christ takes time; we are purified and perfected through the difficulties in Christ, who works everything to the good of those who love him.[51]

However, if we rely purely on our own strength, we will eventually come up against our limitations. For many of us, our faith has never matured, and perhaps many of us have been catechised more by the world than we have by the Church.[52] There could be many reasons for this, but it is never too late to begin again, to go in search of instruction and help. All the sacraments presume faith. It is faith that enables a couple to draw upon the graces made available in the sacrament of marriage. Without living faith, a couple can find themselves living their marriage in a way contrary to the vision of the Church; consequently, they may find themselves obstructing the gifts and the help Christ wants to give to them, without even realising that they are doing so. Faith is, of course, a gift, but the Church promises to grant it to us at our baptism. We however need to nurture it and ensure we place no obstacles in the way; we were created without our consent, but Christ will not redeem us without our co-operation.[53] Christ is the true bridegroom of each one of us, and it is the intimate relationship that both husband and wife have with the true bridegroom that sustains them in their marriage.

> "Could we even imagine human love without the bridegroom and the love with which he first loved to the end? Only if husbands and wives share in that love and in that 'great mystery' can they love 'to the end'. Unless they share in it, they do not know 'to the end' what love truly is and how radical are its demands. And this is undoubtedly very dangerous for them."[54]

The Importance of Fidelity and Indissolubility

With and through Christ the bridegroom, fidelity is possible, marriage vows are sacred, and they underpin the mission of the married couple:

"To bear witness to the inestimable value of the indissolubility and fidelity of marriage is one of the most precious and most urgent tasks of Christian couples in our time...I praise and encourage those numerous couples who, though encountering no small difficulty, preserve and develop the value of indissolubility: thus, in a humble and courageous manner, they perform the role committed to them of being in the world a 'sign' - a small and precious sign, sometimes also subjected to temptation, but always renewed - of the unfailing fidelity with which God and Jesus Christ love each and every human being. But it is also proper to recognize the value of the witness of those spouses who, even when abandoned by their partner, with the strength of faith and of Christian hope have not entered a new union: these spouses too give an authentic witness to fidelity, of which the world today has a great need. For this reason they must be encouraged and helped by the pastors and the faithful of the Church."[55]

Divorce makes present precisely the opposite and contradicts the truth of the Gospel. By definition divorce divides and separates spouses, their children and extended families on both sides and it always will have devastating consequences for all concerned, for society and for the Church. The sign and the image that Christian married couples are called to make present is thereby shattered, defaced, darkened and obscured. For this reason it is a gravely sinful act,[56] the seriousness of which is all too easily obscured in the culture in which we live, a culture that promotes selfish individualism and denies the existence of the one true God: a culture in which divorce is commonplace.

The work of the serpent in the Garden of Eden resulted in the division and separation of God and man, heaven and earth, man's inner integrity, man and woman, and man from the created world.[57] Divorce bears the same hallmark, in that it brings separation and division; it belongs to the kingdom of darkness not to the kingdom of light;[58] it is the work of the father of lies who from the moment of our baptism seeks to rob us of the victory won by the Cross and resurrection of Jesus Christ. The spiritual battle is something very serious for which we need to stay awake:

> "...human nature has not been totally corrupted: it is wounded in the natural powers proper to it, subject to ignorance, suffering and the dominion of death, and inclined to sin - an inclination to evil that is called 'concupiscence'. Baptism by imparting the life of Christ's grace erases original sin and turns man back to God, but the consequences for nature, weakened and inclined to evil, persist in man and summon him to spiritual battle."[59]

Obstacles to Grace
in the Sacrament of Marriage

The Effect of Alternative Worldviews

Appreciating the reality of this spiritual battle, and being prepared to enter it, is vitally important and necessary for every baptised Christian. Married couples need to be particularly conscious of what they need to do to defend their bond. St Paul, in his letter to the Ephesians in which he speaks to married couples defining the meaning of the vocation to marriage, begins by outlining God's eternal plan for man's salvation upon which the sacrament of marriage stands and ends by exhorting the faithful to prepare for the spiritual battle that they will undoubtedly encounter.

> "Put God's armour on so as to be able to resist the devil's tactics. For it is not against human enemies that that we have to struggle, but against the sovereignties and the powers who originate the darkness of this world, the spiritual army of evil in the heavens."[60]

For all, the spiritual battle begins with appreciating that, in addition to the devil, man has two great enemies to fight with - pride and concupiscence. In pride men still seek "to be like gods", and in concupiscence man is tempted to substitute transitory pleasures for true happiness. In both pursuing pride and following the lead of concupiscence, men reject the graces of baptism and of the other sacraments. Very often ideas and ways of living are adopted that are totally contrary to faith and to the Catholic understanding of the human person, of love and of marriage. Many adopt these ideas and attitudes, very often unaware of what they are really doing, or what the consequences will be, especially for marriage.

We live in a society that is rooted more and more in secular and purely humanistic ideology, a society in which the existence of God is at best seriously questioned and at worst denied. The design and plan of God, which guides us on issues of morality and the way to true fulfilment and happiness shown to us through the Gospel, is replaced by humanistic moralism based on reason, and the two cannot and do not equate, despite appearances to the contrary.

> "Consequently, when the sense of God is lost, the sense of man is also threatened and poisoned…when God is forgotten the creature itself grows unintelligible."[61]

Doubt replaces certainty and everybody has their own 'truth'. In consequence, unless we stay very close to Christ through prayer, the Word of God and the sacraments, it becomes increasingly difficult to make sense of ourselves or our lives; then the pressure to adopt secular ways of thinking and being can overwhelm us.

Selfish Individualism
and the Breakdown of Relationship

Individualism, a humanistic and atheistic world view, promotes the subjective goals and values of the individual above any obligation to the community. It is the belief in the primary importance of individual human rights and of self-reliance and personal independence. On the surface, some of these aspirations can appear commendable. Each of us as an individual possesses the dignity of being a person and as such possesses also inalienable human rights; but our dignity as human beings comes from the fact that we are made in the image and likeness of God. We are embodied spirits and as such we are not self-enclosed entities. The call to communion with another and to love is inscribed in our very natures as spiritual beings. We are designed for communion with God and with each other. The notion of defending personal interests regardless of the cost therefore can only divide and separate us. "If we have no peace it is because we have forgotten that we belong to each other."[62]

Individualism finds its roots in a counterfeit freedom: a supposed freedom that comes from independence from God, but is actually "a corruption of the idea and the experience of freedom, conceived not as a capacity for realising the truth of God's plan for marriage and the family, but as an autonomous power of self-affirmation, often against others, for one's own selfish well-being".[63] This sadly is the prevailing cultural atheistic world view which can all too easily creep into the hearts and minds of Christian couples, resulting in conflict, competition and the breakdown of communion.

> "Individualism presupposes a use of freedom in which the subject does what he wants, in which he himself is the one to 'establish the truth' of whatever he finds pleasing or useful. He does not tolerate the fact that someone else 'wants' or demands something from him in the name of an objective truth. He does not want to 'give' to another on the basis of truth; he does not want to become a 'sincere gift'. Individualism thus remains egocentric and selfish."[64]

This separation and division from God and from other people de-personalises us. Individualism does not come from God or his design for the human person, but from sin and from pride. To be a person is to exist in love and this often means denying ourselves for the sake of others, especially our spouse. St Paul in his letter to the Ephesians exhorts married couples to "give way to one another in obedience to Christ."[65] To have adopted the mind-set of individualism and to pursue its aims is to reject the grace given to unite us and instead to seek to reinforce separation from God and others.

34

"For this reason the 'person' is sometimes opposed to the 'individual'…The self-reflective moment which constitutes 'the individual' contributes to the maintenance of the human shape. But the person is only growing in so far as he is continually purifying himself from the individual within him. He cannot do this by force of self-attention, but on the contrary by making himself available and thereby more transparent to himself and others. Things then happen as though the person, no longer 'occupied with himself' or 'full of himself', were becoming able - then and thus only - to become someone else and to enter into grace."[66]

A family, as the first and in a sense the fundamental community for human well-being and flourishing, will thereby inevitably suffer, as husband and wife strive to demand and secure their own individual and independent interests over the interests of their union and communion. Taken to its logical conclusion, this defence of, and insistence on, one's own interests will inevitably lead to marital breakdown and separation. Such a mind-set is thus totally contrary to marriage as the union and communion of persons in love.

True freedom subordinates itself to love, since it is only here that it finds its fulfilment. Thus the man who seeks to love is truly and completely happy to subordinate his freedom to love, because he finds through doing so that he truly discovers himself.[67] He discovers the very meaning of his being and existence by making a sincere gift of himself to others, particularly to his spouse, with whom he can experience true union and communion and happiness.

A Hedonistic Approach

Hedonism is another secular philosophy that promotes a mind-set that ultimately is the very antithesis of that required for true love to grow and mature. It promotes the striving for pleasure and avoidance of pain and consequently as an approach to marriage and family it too has devastating consequences. As already mentioned, the human person, as a result of original sin, suffers the pressure of threefold concupiscence which subjugates him to the pleasures of the senses, to covetousness for earthly goods, and to self-assertion.[68] This is the reality of fallen human nature. Hedonism as a way of life actively pursues these goals.

In choosing to follow Christ, which we do at our baptism and confirmation, and again by entering into the sacrament of marriage, we choose to follow a very different way, one that takes us back to God as our loving father and that sets us free from the power of concupiscence. In co-operation with grace we can truly love God, ourselves and each other, especially our spouse. Pain and suffering take on a new meaning in Christ crucified, and we begin to see that pleasure and submission to instinct do not equate with happiness; the fullness of life lies in taking a different path.

Sacramental marriage is built upon and sustained only by true love: the love of the couple strengthened and renewed in and by Christ. Love is the animating principle of marriage, and the love of the couple, because it is fallen, wounded and fragile, stands in need of purification and healing; in this process, love passes by way of the cross. True love grows and matures through difficulties and self-denial, not through their avoidance.[69]

It is never too late to turn again to Christ, examine our consciences and motivations and seek his help. We need to be deeply convinced that pursing the goals of selfish individualism and hedonism will separate us further from God and from each other, particularly our spouse. Getting our own way and serving ourselves will not ultimately lead us to happiness.[70]

The Eclipse of Sin

Another result of the prevailing secular mind-set is that our modern world no longer speaks of sin, since going along with the temptation to abandon the teaching of the Book of Genesis is the consequent abandonment (for many) of the doctrine of original or personal sin. The Church is accused of having a negative approach to human nature. It is argued that since much of human nature can now be explained in terms of psychological analysis and social conditioning, the concept of sin, whether original or personal sin, is now

an outdated and outmoded way of looking at the world.
Such negativity, it is argued, is detrimental to self-esteem
and to human well-being.

Advances in medical or social sciences are welcomed
by the Church; however she resists the accompanying
proposition that either of these two sciences, or both
together, can explain everything concerned with human
nature or explain all human motivation for behaviour.
Both psychology and social sciences, however useful and
illuminating, if set up as the definitive answer serve only
to obscure the truth concerning personal freedom, which
although wounded by the effects of original sin was not
annihilated, and concerning personal responsibility, which
is inherent to the dignity of the human person. These
contrary ideas and world views have influenced the hearts
and minds of many, including many of the faithful. This
can be seen in the decline in the practice of the Sacrament
of Reconciliation.

What follows from a failure to take sin seriously, to
examine conscience frequently or to take responsibility
for one's actions, is that sacramental confession becomes
redundant and is ultimately abandoned. This then results
in a form of spiritual blindness. Fundamental to any
good relationship, let alone to marriage, is the ability to
acknowledge our faults and to ask for forgiveness. This
awareness and practice in marriage is vitally important. It
is always easy to see the faults of others; but seeing our

own, asking for forgiveness and being open to the graces available in the Sacrament of Reconciliation is something else altogether. It is absolutely necessary to see our own sins because they humble us and give us compassion for one other. When we are blind to our reality of sin yet see the faults of our spouse, our hearts are full of harsh and negative judgements, which, when translated into words and actions, can only do damage to our spouse and to our marriage. Furthermore, if sin is not acknowledged as a serious issue, then neither is the need of a saviour to save us from our sins, and thus our growth in faith is arrested. The decline in church attendance witnesses to this fact. Being convinced and convicted of our sinfulness is the first step in conversion.

As we can see, understanding the role played by sin in our relationships with others and especially as the impetus behind the breakdown of relationships is vital to understanding the truth about the causes of divorce. Hence the rejection of fundamental truths disclosed to us by way of revelation has had serious repercussions for all relationships, but for love and marriage in particular.

The Slavery of Serious Sin and its Effect on Love and Marriage and Communion

"Our hearts are restless until they rest in you."[71] This truth, recognised and experienced by St Augustine, is true for all of us; we journey restlessly seeking happiness and fulfilment, seeking it often in the wrong places - in transitory pleasures and in our own self-aggrandisement through the idolising of money, power or career. The continual making of wrong choices can, however, lead to addiction and slavery to vice. Vice destroys us and those around us, particularly our spouse. Any addiction results in spiritual blindness as to the consequences of these sins and behaviours. Many divorces follow from addiction to pornography, adultery or other seriously sinful sexual behaviours, addiction to alcohol, drugs, the love of money in all of its guises, the idolatry of career and so on.

As men and women we are weak, but when we fall Christ calls us to get back up; to confess, ask forgiveness and start again. When we are addicted to serious sin, greater help is needed; but all our sins were taken to the Cross and destroyed by Christ, and no sin is greater than his love and mercy; he has put an end to sin and death. The devil has been defeated by the death and resurrection of Christ. The first step, therefore, is a return to Christ. Despite our freedom being severely affected by the wound of original sin, it has not been completely annihilated. A choice needs to be made, but it is not the choice to overcome using our own strength but the choice to surrender to the person of Christ in whom everything is possible.

Many make the mistake of trying to manage their situations either by denying them, making excuses, or alternatively by trying to overcome them by their own strength. For too long, perhaps, we have misunderstood what it means to love and behave well, as if it were something we must do entirely of our own resources. A good example is how the parable of the Good Samaritan is often understood. Many of us jump to the conclusion that the only point of the parable is that we should behave and act like the Good Samaritan and love our neighbour in the same way. This aspect of course is true, but it is not the only message of the parable. We cannot give what we do not have; we have first to be healed and enabled to love like this.

The Fathers of the Church always taught that first of all the Good Samaritan is Christ himself,[72] and we, each of us individually, are the person beaten up on the road - having been walking in the wrong direction (the man in the parable was on his way to Jericho, which means he was going away from Jerusalem, the Holy City), beaten up by the world, the flesh and the devil, and left for dead. Those who walk by on the other side and do not stop to help represent the history of the world since the Fall with its cultures and rules, which of themselves cannot bring us the healing that we need or enable us to love. Jesus Christ is the Good Samaritan for us, the one we have been tempted to despise, especially in this modern sophisticated world. He stops and helps us up, attending to our wounds with oil - his love, mercy and forgiveness; and with wine or vinegar - his correction. He picks us up and takes us to the inn - the Church; he pays the full price for our care and restoration to full health - his death and resurrection; and promises to return again and settle up anything else that may be owing - the Second Coming. We can only truly love like this Good Samaritan if we have allowed Christ to love us, heal us and restore us to his Father first. Prayer and the Word of God, catecheses and the sacraments, adoration and the intercession of the saints, point the way forward as does seeking professional help for addictions.

Pride is often our greatest enemy; through it we can often refuse to seek the help of the only one who can truly help us.

> "Such people shun confrontation with a personal God; they evade full avowal of their creaturely status, they balk at that ultimate act of subordination...Nay, they would even surrender to an Impersonal Absolute, to which they would be as parts to a whole and...keep a last remnant of their ego sovereignty...It is only in our confrontation with a personal God that we become fully aware of our condition as creatures, and fling from us the last particle of self-glory."[73]

Christ stands at the door knocking;[74] but what is our response?

> "The situation in which the family finds itself presents positive and negative aspects: the first are a sign of the salvation of Christ operating in the world; the second, a sign of the refusal that man gives to the love of God."[75]

The Effect of Artificial Contraception
on Love and Communion

Living the marital sexual embrace in accordance with its inner truth and beauty is indispensable to sacramental marriage and to creating a true communion of persons. The marital sexual embrace re-affirms the vows and consent of the couple: to give oneself totally, to love faithfully until death and to be open to life. Where artificial contraception is introduced, these vows are directly contradicted, for the gift of self is no longer total and the act is no longer open to life, and as a consequence the promise of fidelity is put at risk.[76]

In God's design there is an inseparable connection between the unitive and procreative significance of the conjugal act.[77] Dividing and separating these two meanings distorts and defaces it; consequently the conjugal act, when artificially deprived of its procreative significance, also ceases to be an act of love.[78] Furthermore the whole sacramentality of marriage rests upon the inseparability of the two meanings,[79] so that to contracept artificially, knowingly and deliberately, is to obstruct and reject the graces made available through the sacrament of marriage and, as we have seen, it is grace that makes it possible for couples truly to love each other "until death does them part". This is something very serious. Many couples, in all honesty, have no idea what they are doing by using contraception; either they have never been told the truth, or perhaps they have never understood it. Sadly, many experience the harmful effects of contraception on their marriage without realising the cause; it is not a coincidence that divorce rates have increased in line with the more widespread use of contraception.[80]

With a return to a relationship of love with God as our Father comes a deep reverence and love for all he has created and ordained. Redemption in Christ includes the redemption of our bodies, not just at the resurrection of the dead at the end of time, but here and now in the rediscovery of the nuptial significance and language of the body, and the ability of married couples to experience true love and communion in marriage as in the beginning. This is the kind of love that is integral to the sacramental sign that they are called to make present in the world.

As we have seen, the father of lies is still active, seeking to deceive, seeking to divide and separate us from the love of God and also from truly loving each other. Blessed John Paul II, when speaking about these issues, describes the marital bedchamber as the place where the forces of good and evil meet and do battle.[81] The marital sexual act of love should be an experience of love involving the body, mind and emotions and the spirit of the person in an integrated way in all truth and beauty and goodness.[82] As men and women in our fallen or disintegrated condition, it is possible for us to experience just the sensual or just the

emotional aspects of love, either together or in isolation; it
is often very difficult for us to ensure that these two aspects
correspond with the third aspect, that of the spiritual truth
of the person and the inner truth and meaning of the act. It is
only when all aspects are acknowledged and respected that
the act can be described as an act of true love. All married
couples are called to learn how to love each other well in
this regard. This process begins with making a conscious
choice in favour of true love and a conscious choice to
co-operate with grace. The way to experiencing this re-
integration of the different aspects of love, and thereby the
meaning of the sexual embrace, lies in following this path.

The ability of man and woman truly to love each other
was not completely suffocated by original sin and its
effects; it is, however, habitually threatened. In the Old
Testament we see examples of true love in the Song of
Songs, the Book of Ruth and the Book of Tobit. In the book
of Tobit we read how Sarah had been given in marriage
seven times, but each time on the night of the wedding
the bridegroom was struck down by a demon before the
marriage was consummated. The archangel Raphael, sent
in disguise to help both Tobit and his family and Sarah and
her family, advises Tobit's son Tobias that he is destined
to marry Sarah. The Latin Vulgate version of Tobit adds
the detail that Tobias asked Raphael how it was that this
demon had power over these men and Raphael explained
that these men had all put God outside of their thoughts at

the time of the consummation of their marriage. Raphael then advises Tobias how to overcome the demon. Tobias follows his advice and he and Sarah entrust themselves to God before consummating their marriage. Through their prayer, God blessed them and protected their union.[83]

Through our baptism and redemption in Christ, a far greater gift is given to us: the possibility of re-reading the language of the body in truth. The Holy Spirit enables us through grace to walk the path towards re-integration, reversing the effects of the Fall. It is Christ himself who protects and purifies our love through the sacrament of marriage, if we too entrust ourselves to him. The marriage bed becomes an altar and the marital sexual act holy; it is an expression of true love made possible through redemption in Christ. This, however, does not happen automatically; we must make a choice, and we must enter the battle for love and purity and co-operate with grace.

St Paul encourages us to "keep the body in holiness and reverence".[84] To be truly human is to be truly integrated in body and soul; experiencing this integration, which begins with our *fiat* to the work of Christ and our co-operating with grace, enables us over time to keep the body "holiness and reverence" as we are called to do. This is what it means to be chaste; the chaste person has chosen to love truly and keep their body in "holiness and reverence". We experience healing and a renewal of our minds as we walk this path and we begin to desire purity of heart and body, since this brings with it a deep serenity and joy that is impossible to experience in any other way. Those who discover this also experience a deep abhorrence towards anything that would distort love and purity.

In many respects, true love is now a task made possible only with grace;[85] this results in re-discovering who we really are, created in the image and likeness of God, and loving therefore in accordance with all truth, beauty and goodness. The discipline of marital fidelity and chastity (which a couple are called to in the vocation of marriage) helps a couple to re-learn how to love well. With regard to conceiving children, the Church teaches that a couple are called to responsible parenthood and are at liberty to space births where there is a serious reason to do so, using methods that reverence and respect God's design, reverence and respect each other, and reverence the gift of their own bodies and sexuality and the gift of fertility.[86]

Because the contraceptive sexual act contradicts and distorts the true meaning of the sexual embrace, rendering it no longer an act of love, such an act will focus on the disordered love of self and on self-gratification.[87] This is an objective fact, regardless of any subjective 'feelings' a couple may have. It is a mutual act of use, not love[88] and a true communion of persons is thereby rendered impossible. In fact, through living this most intimate act in a disordered way the couple risk bringing about its very opposite, that is a further disunity and discommunion between them because this is the nature and effect of evil.

The contraceptive act is an act of irreverence for God as father and creator, and an act of irreverence by husband and wife towards each other. With regard to the latter, it is the woman who is to a greater extent disadvantaged, because men and women experience their fallen sexuality in different ways. Generally speaking, men experience it in a visual and physical or sensual way and for women it is more emotional.[89] Women retain more of the capacity to perceive the other as a person, body and soul after the Fall. She is still entrusted with the care and nurture of the human person,[90] albeit she is reminded of her sin through giving birth amidst pain. She is thus, as a general rule, more sensitive to being used sexually and it is here that the negative and insidious effects of contraception can begin to take their toll on the love between spouses:

> "Another effect that gives cause for alarm is that a man who grows accustomed to the use of contraceptive methods may forget the reverence due to a woman, and, disregarding her physical and emotional equilibrium, reduce her to being a mere instrument for the satisfaction of his own desires, no longer considering her as his partner whom he should surround with care and affection."[91]

Where does such irreverence and disregard come from? It belongs to a world in which man, whether consciously or unconsciously, prefers his fallen state and desires to persist in it. He seeks to continue to be independent of his creator, and persists in wanting to decide for himself what is good and what is evil; thus he rejects the plan and design of God, and inevitably focusses on love of self, not on love and reverence for God or love and reverence for others.

> "In that sin man preferred himself to God...he chose himself over and against God, against the requirements of creaturely status and therefore against his own good...Seduced by the devil, he wanted to 'be like God', but without God, before God, and not in accordance with God."[92]

Such irreverence comes from taking the opposite path to that offered through redemption. The question of contraception in effect involves

> "...a struggle between freedoms that are in mutual conflict, that is, according to the well-known expression of St Augustine, a conflict between two loves: the love of God to the point of disregarding self, and the love of self to the point of disregarding God."[93]

Many couples have been deeply deceived with regard to the issue of contraception. However, it is never too late to go in search of the truth and it is never too late to begin to live our marriages differently and to open ourselves to God's love for us through the Sacrament of Penance. He waits for us as did the father of the prodigal son, who ran to embrace, forgive and re-instate his child into his household, his child who had come to his senses through suffering and hardship and set out truly to seek reconciliation with his father. Many marriages suffer needlessly because of contraception, and many marriages also end in divorce because of its effects.

Marriage under Siege

In many respects marriage and family are under siege from every angle. In Christ, however, there is hope, and for those contemplating divorce the Church would urge reconciliation and repentance.

> "There is no family that does not know how selfishness, discord, tension and conflict violently attack and at times mortally wound its own communion: hence there arise the many and varied forms of division in family life. But, at the same time, every family is called by the God of peace to have the joyous and renewing experience of 'reconciliation', that is, communion re-established, unity restored. In particular, participation in the Sacrament of Reconciliation and in the banquet of the one Body of Christ offers to the Christian family the grace and the responsibility of overcoming every division and of moving towards the fullness of communion willed by God, responding in this way to the ardent desire of the Lord: 'that they may be one.'"[94]

Children of the Bond

Immediately following the discussion with the Pharisees about divorce, children were brought to Jesus, who blessed them and said, "Let the little children alone, and do not stop them coming to me; for it is to such as these that the kingdom of heaven belongs".[95] The tragedy of divorce not only affects the couple involved but also their children; the gravity of its effects can never be underestimated and very often amidst the chaos of the breakdown of marriage it is not easy to see the catastrophic damage being done to the children. The marriage bond is the place ordained by God for the conception, pregnancy and birth of every human being. The child is born of, and is to be nourished by, the loving relationship of his or her parents.[96] In the child the parents are forever 'one body'. Through the bond of love between the parents, the child can find all he or she needs to grow to maturity as a human person and as a Christian. For this educational role the parents are sanctified through the sacrament of marriage.[97]

Divorce shatters the very structure or foundation of the child's origin and intrinsic source of growth, well-being and happiness on every level. The child may well be loved individually by both parents afterwards, but no longer by his or her parents as a couple. By separation or divorce the couple not only leave each other; they also leave their children,[98] even if they remain physically or emotionally close. "It's as if the child had its feet on two tectonic plates separating from each other. He wonders if he will fall into the abyss that grows beneath him. I felt the ground collapse and had the impression I no longer existed."[99]

The child now feels the pressure of being the only link between his parents, since the true link born of the familial structure so fundamental to his identity and security has been broken. In dealing with this, the child is deprived of his or her childhood. The child, not the parent, now feels the pressure of being the guarantor of the bond, as he or she tries in vain to re-establish the familial structure. When they fail, they see the responsibility for the failure as theirs; they blame themselves.[100]

> "He will have to lean upon his own resources, leave his childhood and pass by what he needs to grow, he will pay for it later…for he will lack the resources that every child grows from…basic trust in adults. The loss of basic security creates a vulnerability that resurfaces several years after parental separation."[101]

Divorce usually follows serious marital problems that have proved irresolvable to the couple. These failures and loss of hope deeply affect the child in a negative way, obscuring the truth about their identity, the truth about love, the truth concerning the victory of Christ over sin and death and more seriously the truth about God as a loving father, their loving father.

Many couples have no idea of the damage being visited upon their children. If they were to realise the devastation, perhaps with Christ's help they could find the courage to seek reconciliation and forgiveness so that divorce could be avoided, or at least they could do everything possible to help their children through the pain. Taking this path even if one's spouse does not reciprocate can help to work through the grief and pain. Many parents discover enormous hidden resources of strength born of the desire to defend and protect their children, and with grace this can be the beginning of some sort of recovery. All couples before even contemplating divorce should consider deeply the consequences for their children. A tremendous amount of research is available which makes for sobering reading.[102]

Remarriage

"The man who divorces his wife and marries another is guilty of adultery against her. And if a woman divorces her husband and marries another she is guilty of adultery too."[103]

Anyone (Catholic or otherwise) who obtains a civil divorce and then remarries by way of civil ceremony is objectively committing a grave evil every time they enter into marital relations with this second husband or wife. The Church equates the state of Catholics in this situation with those who are in "manifest grave sin".[104] The Church teaches that the consequence of doing this is to separate oneself from communion with Christ and the Church, and for this reason people in this situation are not permitted to receive the Eucharist.[105]

Many couples find this a hard and difficult teaching, but the Church out of love for them stands firm on this issue.[106] The Church by her action is not condemning these people, she is calling them. When the Pharisees wanted Christ to condemn the woman caught in the act of adultery he did not do so, but neither did he nor could he leave her in a state of serious sin; he called her to come out of it, in the same way that he called Lazarus from the tomb. The wages of sin is death, as St Paul writes, and when we are in a state of mortal sin we have experienced a spiritual death and have lost sanctifying grace. We receive sanctifying grace at our Baptism, but we lose it completely when we commit a mortal sin. We need sanctifying grace to enter eternal life on our death, so to be in this situation of mortal sin is very serious.

Christ said to the woman caught in adultery, "Neither do I condemn you;" but he also added, "go away, and don't sin any more."[107]

We can be so used to hearing commandments as some sort of moralism that we can very easily misunderstand these last few words of Christ and respond negatively with anger, or believe he is just telling the woman that she needs to try harder. When we do this, however, we fail really to hear or understand the true meaning of this Gospel passage. The woman in this moment had a personal encounter with Christ. She experienced his loving mercy for her and also his invitation for her to enter into a personal relationship with him *forever*. He saves her not only from being stoned by the Pharisees but more importantly from her own sinful state. It is his loving her and her experiencing this love that was to enable her to go away and sin no more. His words held a power to bring about what they proclaimed, if she allowed them to find a place in her heart. She would be given the strength in and through him that would enable her to remain faithful. She is loved and cherished by him, and it is this that will now sustain her.

The Mel Gibson film *The Passion of the Christ* captures this very well, for we see the woman again at the time of the crucifixion, together with Mary the Mother of Christ. So struck by Christ is this woman, and so changed, that she is unaware of her own personal safety, she is unafraid of the Roman soldiers and what they might do to her. She stays close to Mary and helps her following the brutal scourging of Christ. Her encounter with Christ replays in her mind and imagination. As he loved her so she loves him in return, to the point of risking everything. The transformation in her is tangible and deeply moving; she is now a faithful disciple. The Church, through her action towards those in a situation of adultery, is seeking to lead them similarly to Christ. The woman caught in adultery was in danger of her life, and it was being made to realise this that opened her to salvation. Those who divorce and remarry whilst the bond of their original marriage remains intact are equally endangering their immortal lives. Being told they are unable to receive the Eucharist is intended to help them to realise the gravity of the situation they are in. The Church therefore loves them by her action, since their choices impoverish them and separate them from the sacramental graces made available in Christ. The Church continues to call couples who divorce or remarry through making "untiring efforts to put at their disposal her means of salvation."[108]

Furthermore, by this action the Church is also loving all her faithful children and protecting them from scandal. Others who might know of a couple's irregular marital situation, and who see them receiving communion, could be led to believe that the Church is condoning their situation. Such couples are excluded, then, to defend all from scandal and the harm that this could cause.

Faith comes from preaching, and salvation begins with repentance and conversion: "Prepare a way for the Lord, make his paths straight".[109] The Church calls all who have divorced and have remarried outside the Church to repentance and conversion; she calls them to come to Christ.

"They should be encouraged to listen to the word of God, to attend the Sacrifice of the Mass, to persevere in prayer, to contribute to works of charity and to community efforts in favour of justice, to bring up their children in the Christian faith, to cultivate the spirit and practice of penance and thus implore, day by day, God's grace."[110]

The Church seeks to help them to see how their choices directly contradict the truth; these choices impoverish them and separate them from Christ. The Church is concerned for their salvation; their salvation is not advanced by re-affirming them in their error, only by calling them out of it as Christ himself did. The final canon of the *Code of Canon Law* (Canon 1752) states that "The salvation of souls, which must always be the supreme law in the Church, is to be kept before one's eyes."

This may seem harsh but to do otherwise in the name of so-called 'pastoral solutions' serves simply to advance a state of sin which can ultimately only do greater harm. A true pastoral approach, therefore, is one that acknowledges the real work of pastors, spoken of at the Second Vatican Council, that of being authentic teachers:

"Teachers endowed with the authority of Christ, who preach to the people entrusted to them the faith to be believed and put into practice; they illustrate this faith in the light of the Holy Spirit, drawing out of the treasury of Revelation things old and new (cf. *Mt* 13:52); they make it bear fruit and they vigilantly ward off errors that are threatening their flock (cf. *2 Tm* 4:1-4)."[111]

It is only the truth that sets us free, and the Church cannot do or say otherwise. Truly loving and truly being concerned for the immortal soul of another means speaking the truth in love.[112] Christ came not to abolish the law but to fulfil it. It is through him that these couples can live faithfully if they choose to do so.

Internal Forum Solution

Where couples who have divorced civilly and remarried are moved to repentance, reconciliation in the Sacrament of Penance is open to them. Reconciliation can only be granted, however, to those who, having repented of breaking the sign of the Covenant and of fidelity to Christ, are also sincerely ready to undertake a way of life that is no longer in contradiction to the indissolubility of marriage. This means, in practice, either leaving the second spouse or, if there are serious reasons for not separating such as children's upbringing, taking on themselves the duty to live in complete continence; that is, abstaining from the acts proper to married couples. This solution, also commonly known as the "brother and sister solution", is also the true meaning of the "internal forum solution". Having had recourse to the internal sacramental forum and being resolved, with the help of God's grace, to live in continence, those concerned may then be admitted to Holy Communion as long as this would not be a cause of scandal.

Many have misunderstood the internal forum solution to mean that where a person is subjectively convinced that their first marriage was invalid they may after discussion with a priest decide for themselves whether or not they may receive the Eucharist. This is however not the teaching of the Church.[113]

Abandoned Spouses who remain Faithful

Many spouses who are abandoned by their husband or wife choose to remain faithful to their wedding vows. These people give an incredible witness to true love and fidelity and have a special place in the heart of Christ and the Church.

> "Loneliness and other difficulties are often the lot of separated spouses, especially when they are the innocent parties. The ecclesial community must support such people more than ever. It must give them much respect, solidarity, understanding and practical help, so that they can preserve their fidelity even in their difficult situation; and it must help them to cultivate the need to forgive which is inherent in Christian love, and to be ready perhaps to return to their former married life.

> "The situation is similar for people who have undergone divorce, but, being well aware that the valid marriage

bond is indissoluble, refrain from becoming involved in a new union and devote themselves solely to carrying out their family duties and the responsibilities of the Christian life. In such cases their example of fidelity and Christian consistency takes on particular value as a witness before the world and the Church. Here it is even more necessary for the Church to offer continual love and assistance, without there being any obstacle to admission to the sacraments."[114]

Invalid Marriage

The Church does not permit divorce, but it does distinguish between valid and invalid marriages. Invalid marriages are those in which, because of some impediment existing at the time of the marriage, one or both of the parties were not free validly to contract marriage in the first place. Those who sincerely believe that their marriage was or is invalid may petition the diocesan tribunal for a declaration that their marriage is null. Until such a declaration is obtained, however, they are presumed to be validly married and are not free to enter into a new marriage. Many couples are deeply convinced that their marriages are invalid; however, by virtue of their choice to be married in Church, their marriage is not their own and it is for the Church to decide ultimately on the issue. For further information please refer to the CTS Explanations booklet entitled *Marriage Annulment in the Catholic Church.*

Pauline Privilege

In certain circumstances the Church permits the dissolution of a purely natural valid marriage; that is, a non-sacramental marriage, where neither party was baptised at the time of the marriage and where during the course of the marriage one of the parties to such a marriage converts and is baptised into the Catholic faith. In such a case, if the unbeliever is not prepared to live peaceably with his or her now believing spouse, the believing spouse can apply to have the marriage dissolved.[115]

> "The rest is from me and not from the Lord. If a brother has a wife who is an unbeliever, and she is content to live with him, he must not send her away; and if a woman has an unbeliever for her husband, and he is content to live with her, she must not leave him…However, if the unbelieving partner does not consent, they may separate; in these circumstances, the brother or sister is not tied: God has called you to a life of peace."[116]

For this privilege to operate, and before any new marriage can be entered into, there must be a questioning of the non-Christian party; after this, in certain circumstances, the baptised person will be permitted to enter a new marriage.[117]

Petrine Privilege

In certain cases involving a marriage between a baptised Christian and a non-baptised person, the Pope (and only the Pope) can grant a decree, at the request of one of the parties to that marriage, dissolving the marriage under what has become known as the Petrine Privilege. The requesting party can be either the baptised party of the earlier marriage, who now wishes to marry another Catholic (or other Christian) in the Catholic Church; or, alternatively, the requesting party is the original non-baptised party to the earlier marriage who now has either been baptised as a Catholic, or if baptised into another Christian Church now wishes to be received into the Catholic Church, or now wishes to marry a Catholic. In the case where the hitherto non-believer makes the request, although the baptism of the previously non-baptised party renders the earlier marriage sacramental, it will only be fully sacramental if it was consummated following that baptism. Provided, therefore, the earlier marriage was not, or has not since become, fully sacramental, it may be dissolved, either on the grounds of it being and remaining a non-sacramental marriage because one of the parties was and has remained unbaptised, or on the grounds that although now sacramental it was never consummated since becoming so, and is therefore not fully sacramental. This privilege may require other conditions to be invoked, and is exercised only rarely.

Permissible Separation

The words in Matthew's Gospel concerning adultery[118] (which do not appear in the other Gospel accounts) have always been understood by the Church to mean that the injured party has a right to separate from the adulterous spouse on account of the adultery, but that the marriage bond would remain intact. This understanding is not excluded from the parallel Gospel texts,[119] and is in line with the teaching of St Paul.[120] In these situations the injured spouse is however encouraged, with the help of Christ, to forgive and be reconciled with their spouse. Whilst separated, neither spouse is free to enter into another relationship.[121]

In this and other certain circumstances, as set out in canon law,[122] the Church whilst upholding the sanctity of the bond will permit physical separation of the spouses. For example, if one of the spouses causes grave mental or physical danger to the other spouse or to their children or otherwise renders common life too difficult, that spouse gives the other a legitimate cause for leaving.[123] In all cases, when the cause for the separation ceases, conjugal living must be restored unless ecclesiastical authority has established otherwise. In these cases, the spouses do not cease to be married and they are not therefore free to enter into a new relationship.

If civil divorce provides the only way to secure protection of children's legal or inheritance rights, then it can be tolerated and will not constitute a moral offence.[124]

The Church encourages spouses in these situations to consider separation only as a last resort and to seek reconciliation by all means and all opportunities open to them. The Church also encourages the whole Church community to support and pray for such couples. We might do this by seeking the intercession of the Blessed Virgin Mary and all the saints, especially those who themselves suffered in their marriages, such as St Rita and St Monica, together with those who by God's grace have reached sanctity in their marriages, such as Blessed Louis and Zélie Martin, parents of St Thérèse of Lisieux, and Luigi and Maria Quattrocchi, the first married couple to be beatified.

Conclusion

"Divorce is immoral because it introduces disorder into the family and into society. This disorder brings grave harm to the deserted spouse, to children traumatized by the separation of their parents and often torn between them, and because of its contagious effect which makes it truly a plague on society."[125]

The truth about divorce is that it is a grave evil, the fruit of sin and of our sinful condition following the fall of man. In Christ we are no longer under the dominion of sin and death unless we choose to be so. Married couples have an amazing mission in the Church which Christ himself enables them to fulfil. Marriage requires a total gift of self to God and to our spouse. In order to gain our lives we must lose them. This is the paradox of the Gospel, and happiness is nowhere else to be found.

"The history of mankind, the history of salvation, passes by way of the family. In these pages I have tried to show how the family is placed at the centre of the great struggle between good and evil, between life and death, between love and all that is opposed to love. To the family is entrusted the task of striving, first and foremost, to unleash the forces of good, the source of which is found in Christ the redeemer of man."[126]

"I think the world today is upside down. Everybody seems to be in such a terrible rush, anxious for greater development and greater riches and so on. There is much suffering because there is so very little love in homes and in family life. We have no time for our children, we have no time for each other; there is no time to enjoy each other. In the home begins the disruption of the peace of the world."[127]

The role of the Church is to announce the Good News of Jesus Christ and to call all men and women to salvation in him and to eternal happiness and peace. God himself gives each Christian a role in this mission, by way of the vocation either to marriage or to the celibate or consecrated life; both vocations are, quite simply, vocations to love. Christ himself equips each person for their task and their mission which cannot be achieved without him.[128] We are always free to accept or reject his call, but our decisions will never be without consequences and those consequences will either be for the good or the ill of ourselves and all those God has entrusted to us.

Further Reading

Catechism of the Catholic Church (second edition, 1997)

Vatican II, *Gaudium et Spes* (CTS Do724)

Vatican II, *Lumen Gentium* (CTS Do726)

Paul VI, *Humanae Vitae* (CTS Do786)

John Paul II, *Evangelium Vitae* (CTS Do633)

John Paul II, *Familiaris Consortio* (CTS S357)

John Paul II, *Letter to Families* (*www.vatican.va/holy_father/ john_paul_ii/letters/documents/hf_jp-ii_let_02021994_families_ en.html*)

John Paul II, *Love and Responsibility* (various editions; most recent, San Francisco CA, Ignatius Press, 1993)

John Paul II, *Man and Woman He Created Them: A Theology of the Body* (translated & introduced by Michael Waldstein; Boston MA, Pauline Books and Media, 2006)

John Paul II, *Veritatis Splendor* (CTS Do616)

Livio Melina & Carl Anderson (eds.), *Oil on the Wounds: A Contemporary Examination of the Effects of Divorce and Abortion on Children and Their Families* (New York, Square One Publishers, 2010)

Endnotes

[1] *Mt* 19:3-9, *Mk* 10:11, 12, *Lk* 16:18. "There exists a clear consensus among the Fathers regarding the indissolubility of marriage. Since it derives from the will of the Lord, the Church has no authority over it. For this reason, from the outset Christian marriage was distinct from marriage in Roman society, even though in the first centuries there did not yet exist any canonical system. The Church in the time of the Fathers clearly excluded divorce and remarriage, precisely out of faithful obedience to the New Testament." Joseph Cardinal Ratzinger *On the Pastoral Care of the Divorced and Remarried,* published by Libreria Editrice Vaticana in the series *Documenti e Studi*, 17.

[2] *Catechism of the Catholic Church* (henceforth *CCC*) par. 2467; John Paul II, *Veritatis Splendor* (henceforth *VS*) 1

[3] John Paul II, *Fides et Ratio* 5

[4] *Fides et Ratio* 5

[5] *Jn* 8:32

[6] *Jn* 18:37

[7] *Mt* 19:3-9

[8] *CCC* 50

[9] *CCC* 51-73

[10] Vatican II, *Gaudium et Spes* (henceforth *GS*) 22 (1)

[11] *Heb* 4:12 *Is* 55:11

[12] *CCC* 374

[13] *VS* 35

[14] *Gn* 2:18

[15] *GS* 24 "Indeed, the Lord Jesus, when he prayed to the Father, 'that all may be one. . . as we are one' (*Jn* 17:21-22) opened up vistas closed to human reason, for he implied a certain likeness between the union of the Divine Persons, and the unity of God's sons in truth and charity. This likeness reveals that man, who is the only creature on earth which God willed for itself, cannot fully find himself except through a sincere gift of himself."

[16] John Paul II, *Familiaris Consortio* (henceforth *FC*) 11

[17] *Gn* 2:24

[18] *Gn* 2:24

[19] John Paul II *Redemptor Hominis,* 10

[20] *Gn* 1:28

[21] *FC* 11

[22] Paul VI, *Humanae Vitae* (henceforth *HV*), 8

[23] *GS* 24

[24] *Mt* 22:37-38

[25] *Gn* 3:5

[26] "I heard the sound of you in the garden...I was afraid because I was naked, so I hid." *Gn* 3:10

[27] *CCC* 398

[28] *Rm* 7:21-23

[29] *Gn* 1:28

[30] *CCC* 377

[31] John Paul II, *Man and Woman He Created Them: A Theology of the Body* (henceforth *MWHCT*) 28:4 (pp.244-245).

[32] *Gn* 3:12,16

[33] *MWHCT* 33 (pp.260-263)

[34] *CCC* 1607

[35] "Our hearts are restless until they rest in you" Augustine, *Confessions* 1.1

[36] *CCC* 377

[37] *CCC* 1606

[38] *MWHCT* 32 (pp.257-263)

[39] *CCC* 1608.

[40] *CCC* 1609

[41] *FC* 3

[42] "But to all who did accept him he gave power to become children of God" *Jn* 1:12

[43] Council of Trent, Session XXIV (*On Holy Matrimony*), par. 2

[44] "By the very fact, therefore, that the faithful with sincere mind give such consent, they open for themselves a treasure of sacramental grace from which they draw supernatural power for the fulfilling of their rights and duties faithfully, holily, perseveringly even unto death. Hence this sacrament not only increases sanctifying grace, the permanent principle of the supernatural life, in those who ... place no obstacle in its way, but also adds particular gifts, dispositions, seeds of grace, by elevating and perfecting the natural powers." Pius XI, encyclical letter on Christian marrage, *Casti Connubii* (31st December 1930) par. 40.

[45] "I am the vine .you are the branches… remain in my love…cut off from me you can do nothing" *Jn* 14:5, 9; *CCC* 1615

[46] "This is because the unbelieving husband is made one with the saints through his wife, and the unbelieving wife is made one with the saints through her husband" *1 Co* 7:14

[47] *LG* 11:2; *CCC* 1641; *MWHCT* 98:8 (p.513)

[48] Council of Trent, Session XXIV (*On Holy Matrimony*), Canon 1.

[49] *Ep* 5:21

[50] *Jn* 17:15

[51] *Rm* 8

[52] *FC* 7

[53] *CCC* 1847

[54] *Letter to Families* 19

[55] *FC* 20

[56] *CCC* 2386

[57] *CCC* 400

[58] *CCC* 1707

[59] *CCC* 405

[60] *Ep* 6:11-12

[61] John Paul II, *Evangelium Vitae* 22

[62] Blessed Mother Teresa of Calcutta

[63] *FC* 6

[64] *Letter to Families* 14

[65] *Ep* 5:21

[66] Emmanuel Mounier, *Personalism*, p.19

[67] *GS* 24

[68] *CCC* 377

[69] Benedict XVI, *Deus Caritas Est* (henceforth *DCE*) 5

[70] *GS* 24

[71] Augustine, *Confessions* 1.1

[72] See the discussion by Pope Benedict XVI in *Jesus of Nazareth* vol.1 (London, Bloomsbury, 2007) chapter 7, pp.194-200.

[73] Dietrich von Hildebrand, *Transformation in Christ* p.156

[74] *Rv* 3:20

[75] *FC* 6

[76] See Janet Smith, *Contraception: Why Not?*, originally a talk given to a meeting of the Catholic Physicians Guild in Columbus, Ohio in 1994; text widely available online.

[77] *HV* 12

[78] "One can say that in the case of the artificial separation of these two meanings (unitive and procreative) in the conjugal act, a real bodily union is brought about, but it does not correspond to the inner truth and dignity of personal communion, '*communio personarum*'. This communion demands, in fact, that the 'language of the body' be expressed reciprocally in the integral truth of its meaning. If this truth is lacking one can neither speak of the truth of the reciprocal gift of self nor the reciprocal acceptance of oneself as a person. Such a violation of the inner order of conjugal communion, a communion that plunges

its roots into the very order of the person, constitutes the essential evil of the contraceptive act." *MWHCT* 123:7, p.633

[79] *MWHCT* 123:6, pp.632-633

[80] Research by One More Soul Inc. - Divorce Rate Graph and History Table available at *http://onemoresoul.com*

[81] *MWHCT* 115:2, p.600

[82] See here John Paul II's earlier book, *Love and Responsibility*.

[83] *Tb* 8:7

[84] *MWHCT* 53:5 quoting *1 Th* 4:3-5

[85] *MWHCT* 59:1, p.360

[86] *HV* 16

[87] "Man can become gift - that is, the man and the woman can exist in the relationship of reciprocal gift of self - if each of them masters himself. Concupiscence, which manifests itself as a constraint '*sui generis*' of the body limits and restricts self mastery from within, and thereby in some sense makes the interior freedom of the gift impossible. ..." (*MWHCT* 32:6)

[88] "...the conjugal act means not only love, but also potential fruitfulness... In the conjugal act it is not licit to separate artificially the unitive from the procreative meaning, because the one as well as the other belongs to the innermost truth of the conjugal act. The one is realised together with the other and, in a certain way the one through the other...Thus in such a case, when the conjugal act is deprived of its inner truth because it is deprived artificially of its procreative capacity, it also ceases to be an act of love." (*MWHCT* 123:6, pp.632-633)

[89] *Love and Responsibility* pp.111-112

[90] *Gn* 4:1-2

[91] *HV* 17

[92] *CCC* 398

[93] *FC* 6

[94] *FC* 20

[95] *Mt* 19:14

[96] Oliver Bonnewijn in Livio Melina & Carl Anderson (eds.), *Oil on the Wounds: A Contemporary Examination of the Effects of Divorce and Abortion on Children and Their Families*, p.51.

[97] *FC* 38

[98] Oliver Bonnewijn in Livio Melina & Carl Anderson (eds.), *Oil on the Wounds: A Contemporary Examination of the Effects of Divorce and Abortion on Children and Their Families*, p.55.

[99] Quoted by Oliver Bonnewijn op. cit. p.50.

[100] Oliver Bonnewijn, as above

[101] Oliver Bonnewijn, op. cit. p.54.

[102] For example, the volume *Oil on the Wounds* cited above.

[103] *Mk* 10:11

[104] *Code of Canon Law* (henceforth *CIC*), Canon 915

[105] *CIC*, Canon 1085 **§1**. A person bound by the bond of a prior marriage, even if it was not consummated, invalidly attempts marriage. **§2**. Even if the prior marriage is invalid or dissolved for any reason, it is not on that account permitted to contract another before the nullity or dissolution of the prior marriage is established legitimately and certainly.

[106] "They cannot receive Eucharistic communion as long as this situation persists. For the same reason they cannot exercise ecclesial responsibilities. Reconciliation through the Sacrament of Penance can be granted only to those who have repented for having violated the sign of the covenant of fidelity to

Christ, and who are committed to living in complete continence." *CCC* 1650

[107] *Jn* 8:11

[108] *FC* 84

[109] *Mk* 1:2

[110] *FC* 84

[111] *LG* 25

[112] "Furthermore, concerning the position of the Magisterium as regards the question of divorced and remarried members of the faithful, it must be stressed that the more recent documents of the Church bring together the demands of truth with those of love in a very balanced way. If at times in the past, love shone forth too little in the explanation of the truth, so today the danger is great that in the name of love, truth is either to be silenced or compromised. Assuredly, the word of truth can be painful and uncomfortable. But it is the way to holiness, to peace, and to inner freedom. A pastoral approach which truly wants to help the people concerned must always be grounded in the truth. In the end, only the truth can be pastoral. 'Then you will know' the truth, and the truth will set you free' (*Jn* 8:32)." Joseph Cardinal Ratzinger, *On the Pastoral Care of the Divorced and Remarried*, published by the Libreria Editrice Vaticana in the series *Documenti e Studi*, 17.

[113] The Congregation for the Doctrine of the Faith's 1994 *Letter to the Bishops of the Catholic Church concerning the Reception of Holy Communion by the Divorced and Remarried Members of the Faithful* says this: "The mistaken conviction of a divorced and remarried person that he may receive Holy Communion normally presupposes that personal conscience is considered in the final analysis to be able, on the basis of one's own convictions, to come to a decision about the existence or absence of a previous marriage and the value of the new union. However, such a position is inadmissible. Marriage, in fact, because it is both the image of the spousal relationship between Christ and his Church as well as the fundamental core and an import in civil society, is essentially a public reality."

[114] *FC* 83

[115] *CIC* Canon 1143 (1) A marriage entered into by two non-baptised persons is dissolved by means of the Pauline privilege in favour of the faith of the party who has received baptism by the very fact that a new marriage is contracted by the same party, provided that the non-baptised party departs. (2). The non-baptised party is considered to depart if he or she does not wish to cohabit with the baptised party or to cohabit peacefully without affront to the Creator unless the baptised party, after baptism was received, has given the other a just cause for departing.

[116] *1 Co* 7:12-15

[117] *CIC* Canon 1146

[118] *Mt* 19:9

[119] *Mk* 10; *Lk* 16

[120] *1 Co* 7:11

[121] *CIC* Canon 1152

[122] *CIC* Canon 1151-1155

[123] *CIC* Canon 1153

[124] *CCC* 2383

[125] *CCC* 2386

[126] *Letter to Families* 23

[127] Blessed Mother Teresa of Calcutta

[128] *Jn* 15:4

Marriage Annulment
in the Catholic Church

Every person, Catholic or not, has the right to petition for a declaration of nullity of his or her marriage. In making such a declaration the Catholic Church states that a particular union was not a valid marriage. Taking full account of the Church's rich teaching on marriage, Stephen Gasche explains why and how in certain circumstances marriages may be annulled. An excellent summary for those seeking advice and for those advising in a pastoral context.

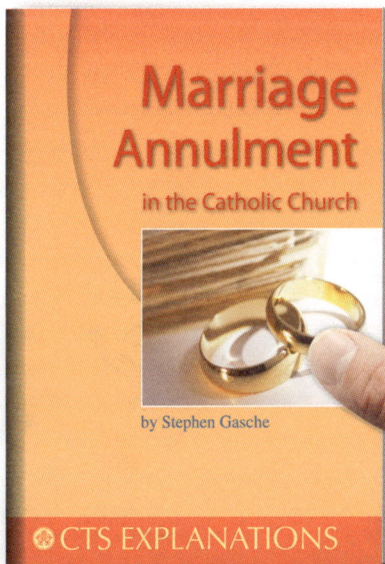

Marriage Annulment in the Catholic Church

by Stephen Gasche

⊚ CTS EXPLANATIONS

Ex 01   ISBN 978 1 86082 039 7

Being a Parent Today

Being a parent today is a huge privilege and a daunting challenge. It raises so many questions about how to love your children, how to live your family life, and how to pass on your Catholic faith. This booklet gathers together the experiences of different mothers and fathers, and some teachers and priests. It is not a list of rules, but a collection of ideas and practical suggestions that will help you reflect on your vocation as a parent and draw closer to your children.

In straightforward language, it deals with topics such as spending time together, listening, discipline, forgiveness, school, prayer, Sunday Mass, sex education, the internet, family celebrations, and much more.

As well as helping individual families, the booklet will be invaluable for parishes and schools that are looking for resources to share with parents.

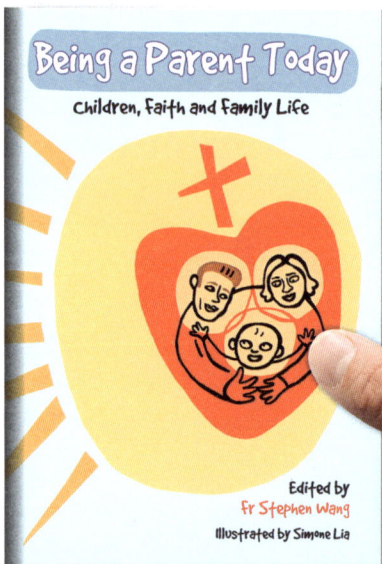

Being a Parent Today

Children, faith and family Life

Edited by
Fr Stephen Wang

Illustrated by Simone Lia

PA 16   ISBN 978 1 86082 786 0